ABC

FROM LAND AND SEA

To Will
Happy 3rd Birthday "
Enjoy your ABC
Irene Kueh

Happy Happy 3rd
Birthday Will
love Grandma &
Poppy

IRENE KUEH & KATHY KESNER

Happy Birthday! :)

Kathy Kesner

ISBN-10:1456450581

ISBN-13:978-1456450588

KATHY'S DEDICATION

For my husband and best friend Bob,
And our precious grandchildren Keyona, Cooper, and Taylor.
You have brought so much joy to my life!

To all of God's creatures that I've ever known, loved, or lost;
With special thanks to their Creator.
You all live on in my memories.
(I miss you still, my sweet Shelby girl)
Your unconditional love was just a glimpse
of the love our Heavenly Father has for us.

Thank you.

IRENE'S DEDICATION

This book is for all of you animal lovers out there
Especially My Mom Annie Soh & Dad Bernard Kueh

&

In loving memory of my best friend Lane
And all best friends that once filled my life
And now forever live in my heart

ABC

FROM LAND AND SEA

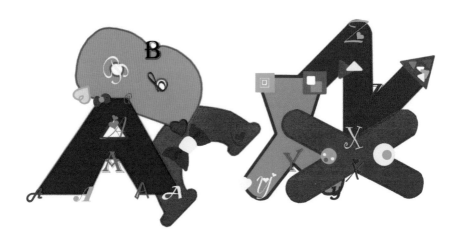

I love to learn my A B C's

I love to learn my X Y Z's

With my friends from land and sea

You will love it, too. You'll see!

A

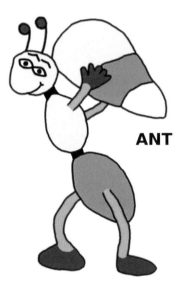

ANT

I'm the most diligent of my kind, I'd say

I work very hard night and day

I'll stop and help a friend along the way

I'm determined and loyal come what may

B

BUTTERFLY

In the pretty garden and sky so blue

Tiny wings flutter through and through

Dancing, waltzing like bumble bees do

Lively, jolly, and bubbly, too

C

CAT

I meow for food

I meow for drink

I meow for affection

Or so you think!

D

DOG

I have four legs

And a tail to wag

I love to run

Come! Let's play tag.

E

ELEPHANT

I am a very large mammal and also grand

I roam free in African and Asian land

I have one strong trunk and four long teeth

And two sharp tusks that are underneath

F

FOX

People say be careful, I'm so sly

I really do not understand why

I'm so cute and oh so shy

People are jealous, perhaps that's why.

G

GIRAFFE

I am the tallest animal you'll ever see

My neck and legs distinguish me

My friends and I like to play

On the plains and in the forests every day

H

HORSE

I love to trot in the fields so green

I love to gallop, it's a beautiful scene

When I canter I put on a show

I also may walk just easy and slow

I

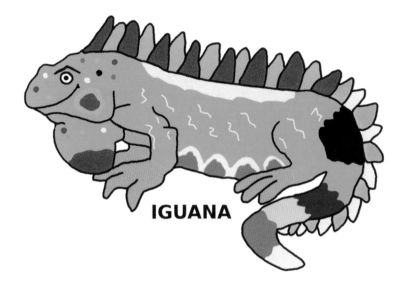

IGUANA

I am a type of lizard, an exotic reptile

On land and water, I am fast and agile

I have a good sense of hearing, sight, and smell

I have sharp teeth and claws that work quite well

J

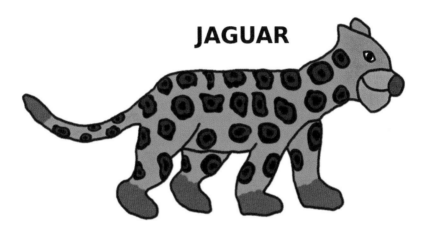

JAGUAR

Of all the wildcats big and strong

At the top of the class is where I belong

When you see my big feet and the size of my head

It's very surprising how softly I tread

K

KANGAROO

I am the world's largest living marsupial

I am usually found on Australia's soil

With my strong legs I hop, with my tail I steer

I've a powerful kick. Don't come too near!

L

LION

As everyone knows, I'm King of the Beasts

Respected by all from greatest to least

I rule my kingdom with a mighty ROAR

My mane's like a crown. That's what it's for.

M

MOUSE

I may be tiny

But why should I worry?

'Til I see Mr. Cat

Then watch me scurry.

N

NIGHTINGALE

I'm a bird with brown feathers and a reddish tail

Wherever I perch, I sing without fail

I am well known for my sweet melodic call

Once they hear me sing, I'm loved by all

O

A hunter, a watcher, a listener so wise

I look all around with my staring eyes

You may hear me hoot in the dark of night

When I spread my wings, it's an awesome sight

P

PENGUIN

How cute am I with my black and white feathers

They keep me warm in the cold Arctic weather

My short and stout arms are really flippers

I swim so fast you'll call me a "zip"per

Q

QUAIL

I am a bird so small and plump

With a plume on my head in a dark little clump

I lay my eggs in a nest on the ground

I hide it well so they can't be found

R

RABBIT

I love to leap and skip and hop

Once I get going I'm hard to stop

Or you might see me sitting in your yard

Still as a statue. Look real hard!

S

SNAIL

I can be found in the garden, the river and sea

My body is long, moist and slimy

My shell is hard, it protects my soft body

I love to wander when it's cold and cloudy

T

TORTOISE

My home is my shell

It's shaped like a dome

I'm slow, can't you tell?

That's the end of my poem

U

UNICORN

Many say I'm not real, I don't exist

I'm a legendary animal, a mythical beast

I look like a horse with a horn on my crest

Mysteriously enchanting, I think I'm the best.

V

VULTURE

I'm a big bird of prey with a strong hooked beak

My head is bald. Come take a peek.

With my wide wingspan and muscular feet

I circle the sky searching for meat.

W

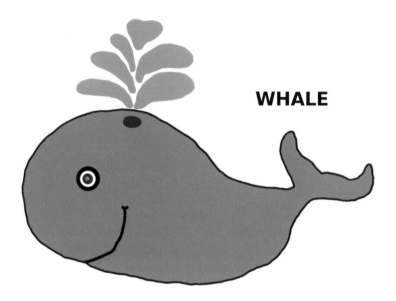

WHALE

I'm a very large mammal living in the sea

My blowhole gets some air to me.

I can jump out of the water and twirl around

I love to sing. I'm the loudest around.

X

X-RAY FISH

I'm a transparent fish like an x-ray

My bones are visible for display

I'm adaptable, pleasant, friendly, and tiny

When I swim in your tank, I'm very shiny

Y

YAK

I look much like a giant ox

My horns are long and massive

My legs are stocky. I'm built like a box.

I can be mean or passive.

Z

ZEBRA

I look like a horse wearing black and white stripes

I'm very unique, no two are alike

Roaming around, spending time with my friends

We run and play until the day ends

KATHY'S LAST RHYME

Irene birthed this book; then dragged me in, too.
She asked me to "tweak" it; make it special for you.
I kicked and I screamed and I tried to run.
Thanks to her for the push. It's really been fun!

* *

IRENE'S SCRIBBLE

ABC FROM LAND & SEA started when a friend asked me to take a look at his poetry. It inspired me and soon after, this book was born. So, Keirse Knight, Thank You. And Thank You, Kathy Kesner. Without Kathy's amazing imagination, it is not possible for me to make you and your child smile. Didn't you smile when you read her last rhyme? I now I did! I look forward to future writings with Kathy. Also, I've ever drawn cartoons in my life and this is my first attempt. I learned om the web. So, thank you to all the 'Teachers' out there.

in line, I must thank Mom Annie Soh and Dad Bernard Kueh. My or animals was sown by them. My childhood house was once to many stray and injured animals. All of them became good hat I will cherish forever in my heart.

nk You to all animal lovers around the world. To name a few:
: Veronica, Shirley & Dennis & Immanuel Shelden & Baby,

Francis; The Muellers: Don & Spaz (Thank You for your patience and moral support), Yvonne (Thank you for everything!), Gloria, Larry & Karen, Dave & Camille, Doug & Michelle & Austin, Dan & Lori & Kristyn & Kayla & Kelli; The Sohs: Grandma Agnes, Aunty Lily & Family, Stephen & Stanley, Annie & Raymond; Doug Reinking & The Gals: Amy Eads, Angie Ritchhart, Connie Tammeus, Debbie Gleason, Kari Hutchison, Kim O'Donohue, Laural Sutton, Linda Webster, Lori Willis, Melissa Cathers, Sheryl Eaton, Sue Mote & Tana Pullen; Friends & Family: Andrew Walker, Cato Thoresen, Cheryl Leasure & Jessica Evans, Christian Otrel, Christine & Scott Rupert, David Terrace, Dawn Bertolinni, Debbie Riggins, Don Hanchett, Erin Eskra, Eunice Tay, Jens Huseby, Joanne & Keith & Jeremiah Schmidt, Karen Kho, Kathy & Bob Kesner, Kristoffer Skaven, Margarita Naming & Nolan Chee, Monica Yap, Patricia Lim & Alex & Liam O'Callaghan, Paul & Kathy & Jon & Rob Emory, Sabine Caroline & Peter Rochel, Shafilda Jane & Andrew & Lea Kristina & Karson Jacob Miles & Baby.

A special THANK YOU to Dr. Ron Pierce & his staff at Best Friends Animal Hospital. Like my parents, their actions speak volumes. Thank you for taking good care of my best friend Lane to his very end.

Last but never the least, I thank God for everything He has given me and this Earth! Everyone I meet along the way is a gift from Him. Every animal I touch and see and read about is His present to me. Especially these two friends He sent my way: Lane & Spaz. THANK YOU!

Peace!

Made in the USA
Charleston, SC
20 May 2011